Earth:
The Water Planet

by E.C. Hill

Table of Contents

Pictures To Think About

ARCTIC
OCEAN

NORTH
AMERICA

ASIA

N

W   E

S

PACIFIC
OCEAN

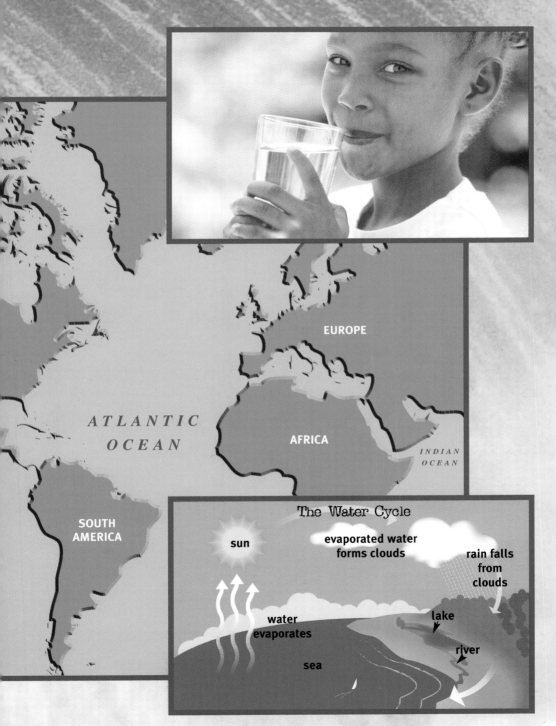

EUROPE

ATLANTIC
OCEAN

AFRICA

INDIAN
OCEAN

SOUTH
AMERICA

The Water Cycle

sun

evaporated water
forms clouds

rain falls
from
clouds

water
evaporates

lake

river

sea

Words To Think About

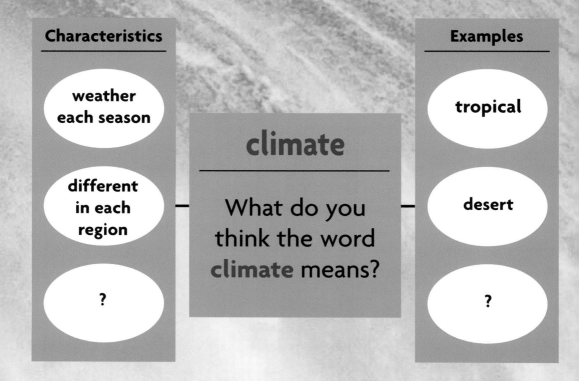

Characteristics

- weather each season
- different in each region
- ?

climate

What do you think the word **climate** means?

Examples

- tropical
- desert
- ?

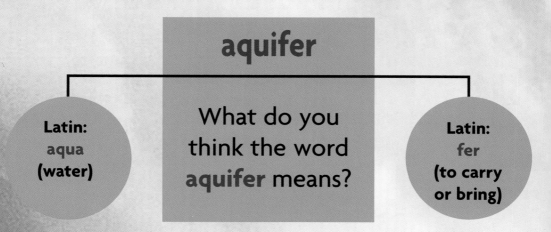

aquifer

What do you think the word **aquifer** means?

Latin: aqua (water)

Latin: fer (to carry or bring)

Read for More Clues

aquifer,   page 22
climate,   page 3
spring,   page 19

spring

What do you think the word **spring** means in this book?

Meaning 1
to leap
or jump
(verb)

Meaning 2
season
of the year
(noun)

Meaning 3
a place where
water comes
from underground
(noun)

Introduction

All living things need water to live. You do, too. Your body is made mostly of water. More than 65% of the human body is water.

Water is everywhere. You can find water in many places on Earth. In fact, if you were in space looking at Earth, you'd see mostly water.

▲ This watering hole is in Etosha National Park, Namibia.

Read this book to learn more about water. See how it shapes our planet. Find out about the oceans. Learn how oceans affect the world's **climate**. Then learn about fresh water. Find out where it comes from and how we use it.

Oceans

Water covers most of Earth. Most of that water is in the oceans. The Earth has four oceans. They are the Pacific, Atlantic, Indian, and Arctic Oceans.

Ocean water is called salt water. Ocean water is about 3.5% salt. You can taste the salt in ocean water.

They Made a Difference

Otis Barton and William Beebe were the first people to go to the deepest parts of the ocean. The two men made a bathysphere to take them into the deep sea. It looked like a steel ball with a window in it. The two men used it to dive more than 3,000 feet (914 meters) into the ocean.

1. Solve This

The Pacific Ocean is approximately what fraction of the world's oceans? Hint: This is a two-step problem. First you have to add together all the oceans. You can estimate to get an approximate answer.

▲ **Over 70% of Earth's surface is covered by water.**

Oceans

Ocean	Size
Pacific Ocean	70,000,000 square miles (181,299,167.7 sq km)
Atlantic Ocean	31,830,000 square miles (82,439,321.6 sq km)
Indian Ocean	28,350,000 square miles (73,426,162.9 sq km)
Arctic Ocean	5,440,000 square miles (14,089,535.3 sq km)

The Ocean Floor

The ocean floor is just like land. The ocean floor has mountains, valleys, hills, and plains. We can't see them because they are hidden by water. Let's look under the water. Let's look at the ocean floor.

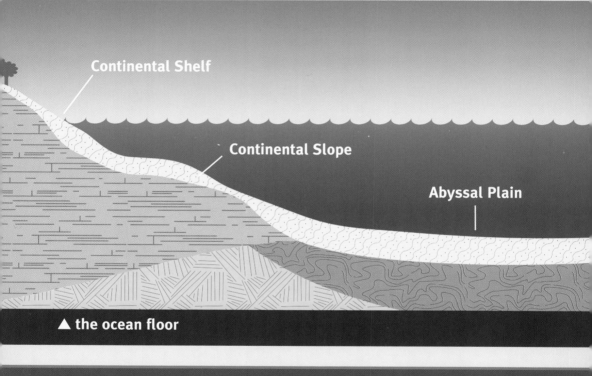

Continental Shelf

Continental Slope

Abyssal Plain

▲ the ocean floor

It's a FACT

The highest point on Earth is Mount Everest. The lowest point in the oceans is in the Marianas Trench in the Pacific Ocean. The longest mountain range is under the ocean. It is called the mid-ocean ridge. It runs for more than 50,000 miles (80,467.2 kilometers).

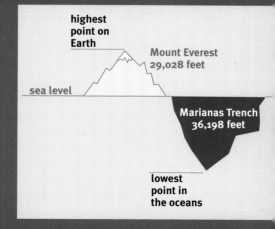

highest point on Earth

Mount Everest 29,028 feet

sea level

Marianas Trench 36,198 feet

lowest point in the oceans

The ocean floor has three parts. The ocean floor gets deeper very slowly around the edges of a continent, or large mass of land. This part is called the **continental shelf**.

Then the continental shelf ends. The ocean floor drops and forms a steep slope. This slope is called the **continental slope**.

The continental slope goes very deep very fast. Then the slope becomes flat. This flat part is called the **abyssal plain** (uh-BIS-uhl PLAYN). The abyssal plain covers almost one-half of Earth's surface.

▲ Have you ever been to an ocean beach? When you walked into the water, you were on the continental shelf.

Oceans on the Move

Have you ever been hit by a wave? What makes waves? What makes ocean water move? The sun makes the ocean move. How does it do that?

First, the sun heats the air over the ocean. Warm air is lighter than cold air. The warm air rises. Then cooler air flows in to replace the warm air. This makes wind. Whoosh!

Wind blowing on the surface of the ocean makes waves. The harder the wind blows, the bigger the wave.

▲ Waves moving toward the shore must travel uphill.
(Remember the continental shelf.) That's why the

Everyday Science

Ocean water contains many minerals. The main mineral is sodium chloride. That's the salt people put on food.

Currents

Wind blows over the ocean day after day. During the day, wind blows from the water to the land. At night the wind blows the opposite way. At night it blows from land to water. The wind makes the oceans move in strong currents. A current is like a river that flows through the ocean.

Currents flow in all oceans. Currents carry cold water to warm regions. They also carry warm water to cold regions. Most currents move in circles.

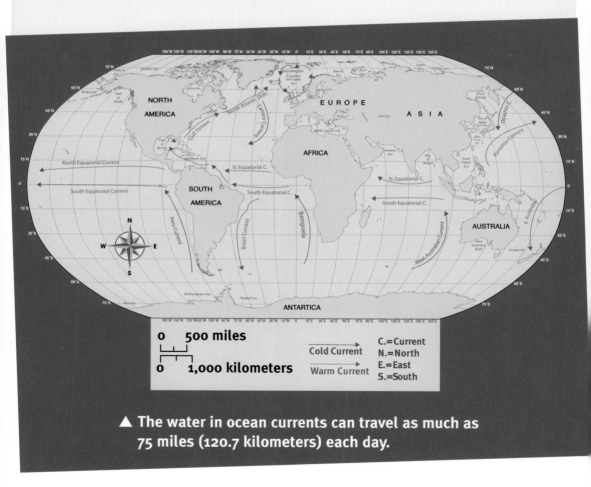

▲ The water in ocean currents can travel as much as 75 miles (120.7 kilometers) each day.

The Gulf Stream is a major ocean current. The Gulf Stream starts in the warm waters near Florida. Then it moves northeast across the Atlantic Ocean. It brings warm water to northwestern Europe. The Gulf Stream warms that region's climate.

It's a FACT

Benjamin Franklin discovered that the fastest way to sail from America to England was to use the Gulf Stream. His discovery sped up the delivery of mail between America and Great Britain.

▲ Palm trees grow along the southwest coast of Great Britain. The Gulf Stream warms this area enough for palm trees to grow here.

Weather and the Water Cycle

It is a hot day. You swim in a pool. You get out and walk to your towel. You leave wet footprints as you walk. In a minute your footprints are gone. Where did they go?

The heat caused the water to **evaporate**. Liquids like water turn into **vapor**, or gas, when they evaporate. The water in your footprints turned into gas and floated away.

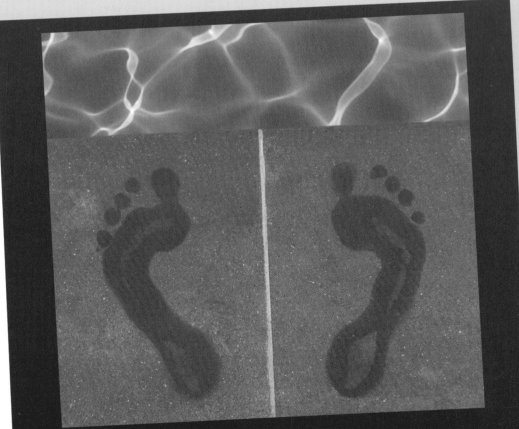

▲ The hot sun will make these wet footprints evaporate quickly.

The same thing happens with oceans and other bodies of water. The sun heats the water. Then a lot of water evaporates. The water vapor rises into the air. The vapor forms clouds.

Sometimes rain falls from the clouds. Rain falls when the water droplets in the clouds become very heavy.

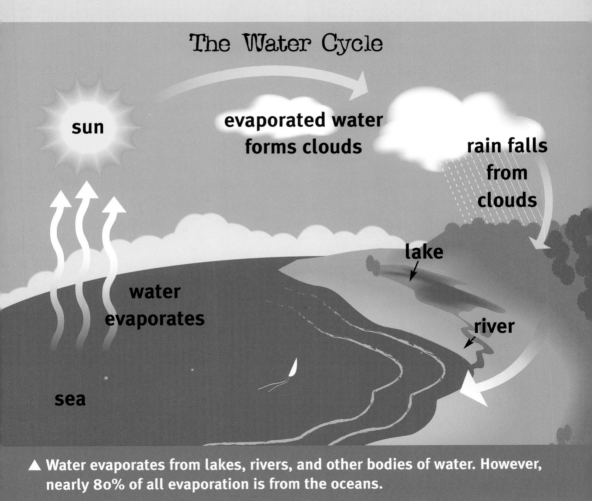

The Water Cycle

sun

evaporated water forms clouds

rain falls from clouds

lake

water evaporates

river

sea

▲ Water evaporates from lakes, rivers, and other bodies of water. However, nearly 80% of all evaporation is from the oceans.

Some places get lots of rain. Wind and rain follow patterns. A pattern does the same thing each time. One wind pattern is a **monsoon**. Monsoons affect India and Asia during the summer.

Every summer, strong winds blow over the Indian Ocean. Moist air from the ocean forms clouds over the land. Then heavy rain falls in parts of India and Asia.

▲ Some of the wettest places on Earth are in India. Some areas get over 400 inches (1,016 centimeters) of rain in an average year.

Clouds and the Wind

Clouds are almost always moving. The wind moves the clouds. Remember that clouds are full of water. When you watch clouds move, you are also watching water move.

Sometimes the water stays in the clouds for days. Other times it falls as rain. What makes the rain fall to the ground? Read on to find out.

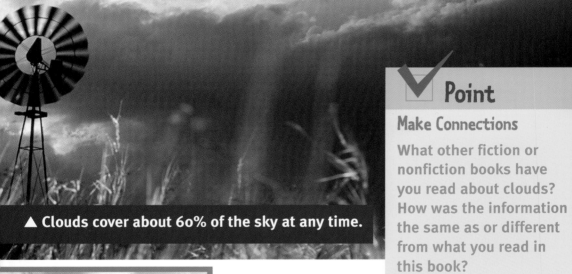

▲ Clouds cover about 60% of the sky at any time.

✔ Point

Make Connections

What other fiction or nonfiction books have you read about clouds? How was the information the same as or different from what you read in this book?

Careers in Science

Do you wonder what causes the weather? Then being a climatologist might be the job for you. Climatologists are scientists who study the climate. They gather information about the world's weather and the causes of weather patterns. Climatologists are worried that Earth's climate is changing in many ways.

Completing the Water Cycle

The sun is a great force. The sun's heat moves water around the planet. There is another force that moves water, too. This force is called **gravity**. Gravity is a force that pulls things toward the center of Earth.

Drop a ball and it falls to the floor. Gravity pulls the ball to the floor. Gravity also makes rain fall. Gravity pulls rain to the ground.

It's a FACT The amount of water in the planet's water cycle never changes. The water that falls as rain or snow has existed for billions of years. It has moved through the water cycle countless times.

▲ Storms like hurricanes carry large amounts of water from the sea to the land.

Most rain sinks into the ground. Sometimes there is too much rain. Where does that water go? That water becomes **runoff**. Runoff is water that flows over the surface of land into streams and rivers.

Gravity pulls the water in streams and rivers downhill.

The water keeps flowing downhill until it reaches the lowest point. Many rivers flow into oceans. When the river water reaches the ocean, it completes the water cycle. Then the water cycle starts all over again.

✔ Point

Reread

Reread page 13 to find out where the water in clouds comes from.

▲ Salak River in Borneo

Fresh Water

The water we drink is fresh water. Fresh water is not salty like ocean water. When water evaporates, the water vapor is pure. The salt does not evaporate with the water. This is why rain water is fresh water.

Many lakes hold fresh water. Lakes are bodies of water surrounded by land. Ponds also hold fresh water. Ponds are like lakes, except smaller.

▲ There are millions of lakes in the world. Canada alone has about two million.

Water from streams and rivers flows into lakes and ponds. Water also flows up from **springs**. Springs are places where water flows up from underground.

Lake Superior is one of the Great Lakes. It is also the largest fresh water lake in the world. Another lake holds even more fresh water. Lake Baikal in Asia is deeper than Lake Superior. Lake Baikal isn't as wide as Lake Superior, but it holds more water.

Lake	Depth
Superior	1,333 feet (406 meters)
Baikal	5,370 feet (1,637 meters)

▲ Lake Superior is the deepest of the Great Lakes. Lake Baikal is about four times as deep.

It's a FACT

Animals are mostly made of water. Plants also contain plenty of water. Even the driest plants are about 50% water. All living things need water to survive.

19

Rivers

Rivers are different from lakes. Lakes hold water. Rivers move water. Water flows down rivers. Some rivers move fast, and others move slowly.

Many rivers start high in the mountains. Often they start as streams. Streams rush downhill from the high ground. When many streams come together, they become a river.

2. Solve This

How much longer is the Nile River than the Yangtze River?

▲ Yangtze River

The World's Longest Rivers

River	Length
Nile (Africa)	4,100 miles (6,598.3 km)
Amazon (South America)	4,000 miles (6,437.4 km)
Mississippi/Missouri (North America)	3,800 miles (6,115.5 km)
Yangtze (Asia)	3,700 miles (5,954.6 km)
Yenisei (Asia)	3,400 miles (5,471.8 km)

Let's look at the Amazon River. It is one of the longest rivers in the world. The Amazon starts as a small stream high in the Andes Mountains. The stream moves very fast downhill. Other streams join it. Together the streams become larger and larger. More than 1,000 streams pour water into the Amazon. That is why the Amazon is such a mighty river.

✔ **Point**

Visualize

Use the information on this page to draw what you think the Amazon looks like at its beginning.

▲ The Amazon River holds nearly one-fifth of the river water in the world.

Underground Water and Ice Caps

You can find fresh water in two other places. Each of these places holds more fresh water than all the lakes and rivers combined.

The first place is under the ground. Rain water sinks into the earth. Some of the water passes deep into the layers of sand and rock. That water builds up after thousands of years. Huge amounts of water are underground. The layers that hold underground water are called **aquifers** (AHK-wuh-fuhrz).

▲ The Ogallala Aquifer is an important source of underground water. It's found under the Great Plains of the United States.

You can also find fresh water in very cold places. Ice is a form of fresh water. Places such as Antarctica and Greenland are covered in layers of ice. These layers of ice are called **ice caps**. Ice caps form when snow builds up. Over time, the snow becomes packed into layers of ice.

The ice caps in Antarctica are nearly 3 miles (4.8 kilometers) thick in places. Some of this ice may be over 400,000 years old.

▲ Glaciers form the same way ice caps do. Many glaciers are found in high mountains, where snow builds up over time.

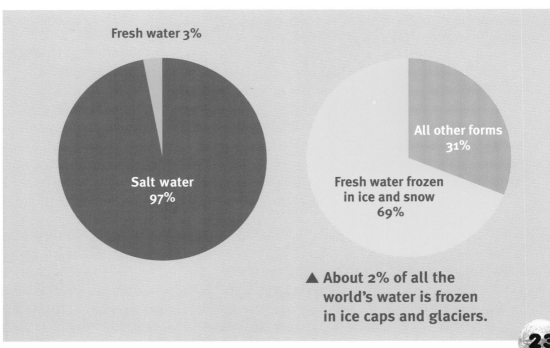

Fresh water 3%

Salt water
97%

All other forms
31%

Fresh water frozen
in ice and snow
69%

▲ About 2% of all the world's water is frozen in ice caps and glaciers.

23

Using Water

We use water every day. We drink water. We wash with water. We even cook with water.

Farmers use water to grow food. Farmers also give water to the animals they raise.

Can you think of other ways we use water every day?

It's a FACT People in the United States use a lot of water. For drinking, cooking, washing, and flushing, Americans use seventy-four gallons of water per person every day.

3. Solve This

In which way do Americans use the most water? Which use is just over 1/5 of the total?

How Do Americans Use Water?

Kitchen 5%

Cleaning (washing machines, etc.) 21%

Bathroom 74%

When you turn on a light, you may be using water. Dams on rivers can make electricity. The dams use special machines to make electricity. The machines are called **turbines**. Turbines use the flow of water to make electricity.

Water has another important use. Water is also fun! Many people around the world enjoy fishing, sailing, and swimming in water.

▲ Millions enjoy lakes in the summer. Some even fish on frozen lakes in the winter.

▲ Rivers flowing into Canada's Hudson Bay are dammed to produce electricity.

Overuse

People do not always use water wisely. People need to learn to use water so that it lasts.

People in cities use a lot of water. After the water is used, the water is dirty. The dirty water is called wastewater.

In the past, cities dumped the wastewater into the rivers or the oceans. This was not good. Today, many cities clean the water before it is dumped.

◀ Israel has a dry climate. That's why it uses all the available fresh water to meet its needs.

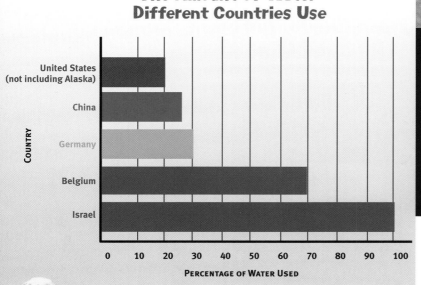

The Amount of Water Different Countries Use

COUNTRY

- United States (not including Alaska)
- China
- Germany
- Belgium
- Israel

0 10 20 30 40 50 60 70 80 90 100

PERCENTAGE OF WATER USED

Water can be overused. Water from deep underground is pumped to the surface. Farmers in the United States use this water every day. Rain replaces the water but it takes a long time. Wells can go dry when too much water is used too quickly.

The Aral Sea

▲ The Aral Sea in central Asia was once the fourth largest lake in the world. The sea has shrunk and split into several smaller lakes. Scientists worry that it may disappear completely in the future.

27

Water and the Future

The world's population is growing fast. More and more people will need water. They will need it for drinking, washing, and growing food.

Water is a limited resource. A resource is something that is valuable to a person or place. The world has only so much water to share. What can people do to save water?

 The Florida Everglades are natural wetlands. They once covered more than four million acres. Today they cover only half that much land. Now people are buying back land that was turned into farms. They plan to make the land part of the Everglades again.

Wetlands are one answer. These low, marshy areas make water cleaner. Wetlands do this by filtering out waste. Some towns have created wetlands to treat wastewater.

Wetlands are also home to many plants and animals. People can visit them to enjoy nature. Building and restoring wetlands helps us all save water.

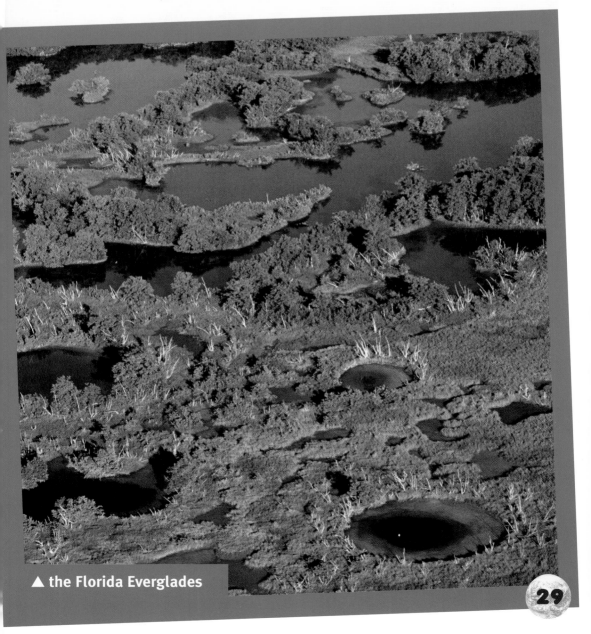

▲ the Florida Everglades

Conclusion

Earth holds a lot of water. Most of the water is in the oceans. The oceans are salt water. Ocean water evaporates and forms clouds. Rain and snow fall from clouds.

Rain and snow bring fresh water to the land. Lakes and rivers have fresh water. Fresh water is also found underground and in ice caps.

People use fresh water for drinking, washing, and growing food. We cannot live without water.

Water is a limited resource. It renews itself very slowly. People must use water wisely.

Water	
Salt water	in oceans
Fresh water	in lakes, rivers, aquifers, and ice
People use water	in many ways

Glossary

abyssal plain	(uh-BIS-uhl PLAYN) the vast floor of the deep ocean (page 7)
aquifer	(AHK-wuh-fuhr) an underground layer of sand, gravel, or stone that contains water (page 22)
climate	(KLIGH-mit) the average weather conditions of a place or region throughout the year (page 3)
continental shelf	(kon-tuh-NEN-tuhl SHELF) the gently sloping part of a continent that is under water (page 7)
continental slope	(kon-tuh-NEN-tuhl SLOHP) the edge of a continent that drops steeply down to the deep ocean floor (page 7)
evaporate	(i-VAP-uh-rayt) to become a vapor, or gas (page 12)
gravity	(GRA-vih-tee) the force that pulls objects toward the center of Earth (page 16)
ice cap	(ICE KAP) a thick layer of permanent ice (page 23)
monsoon	(mon-SOON) a very strong wind that blows in the Indian Ocean and southern Asia (page 14)
runoff	(RUN-off) rain that flows over the ground and into streams (page 17)
spring	(SPRING) a place where underground water flows out of the ground (page 19)
turbine	(TUR-bighn) a machine that uses the power of flowing water to make electricity (page 25)
vapor	(VAY-puhr) a gas that can be seen in the air, like mist, steam, or smoke (page 12)

Answers to Solve This

Page 5: a little more than one-half

Page 20: 400 miles (643.7 km)

Page 24: bathroom; cleaning

Index